Statuesque

adult coloring book

by

Tabz Jones

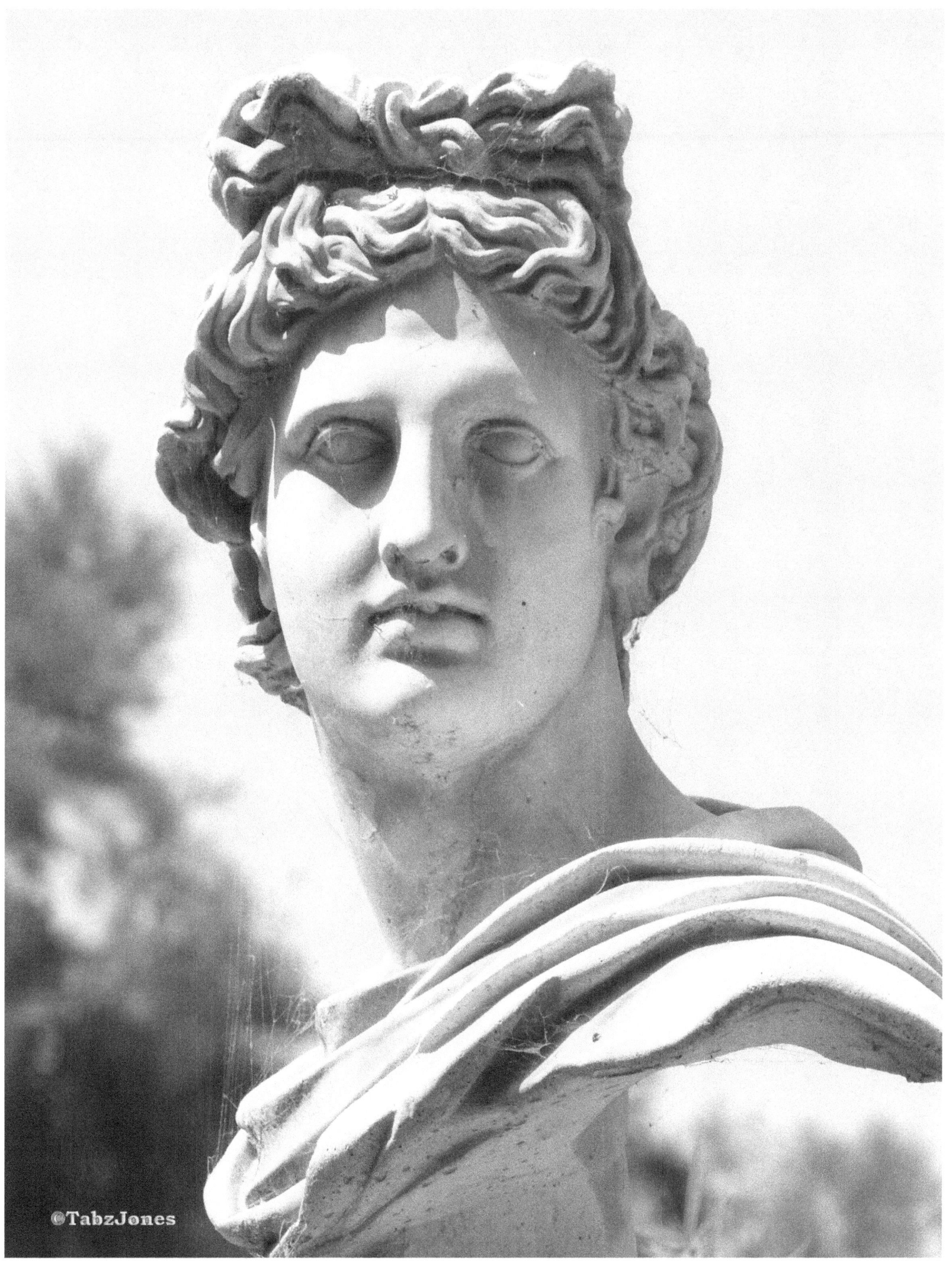
@TabzJones

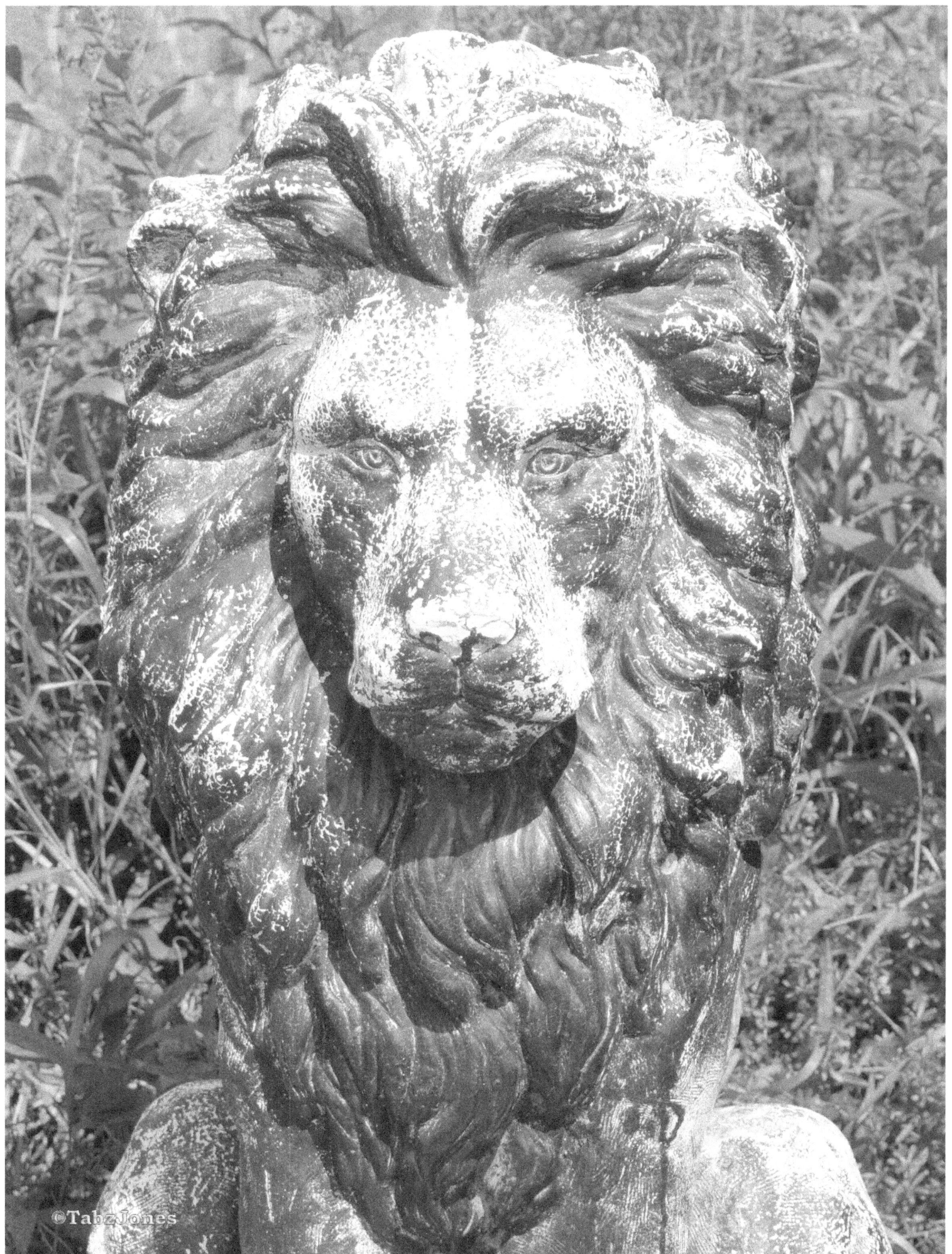

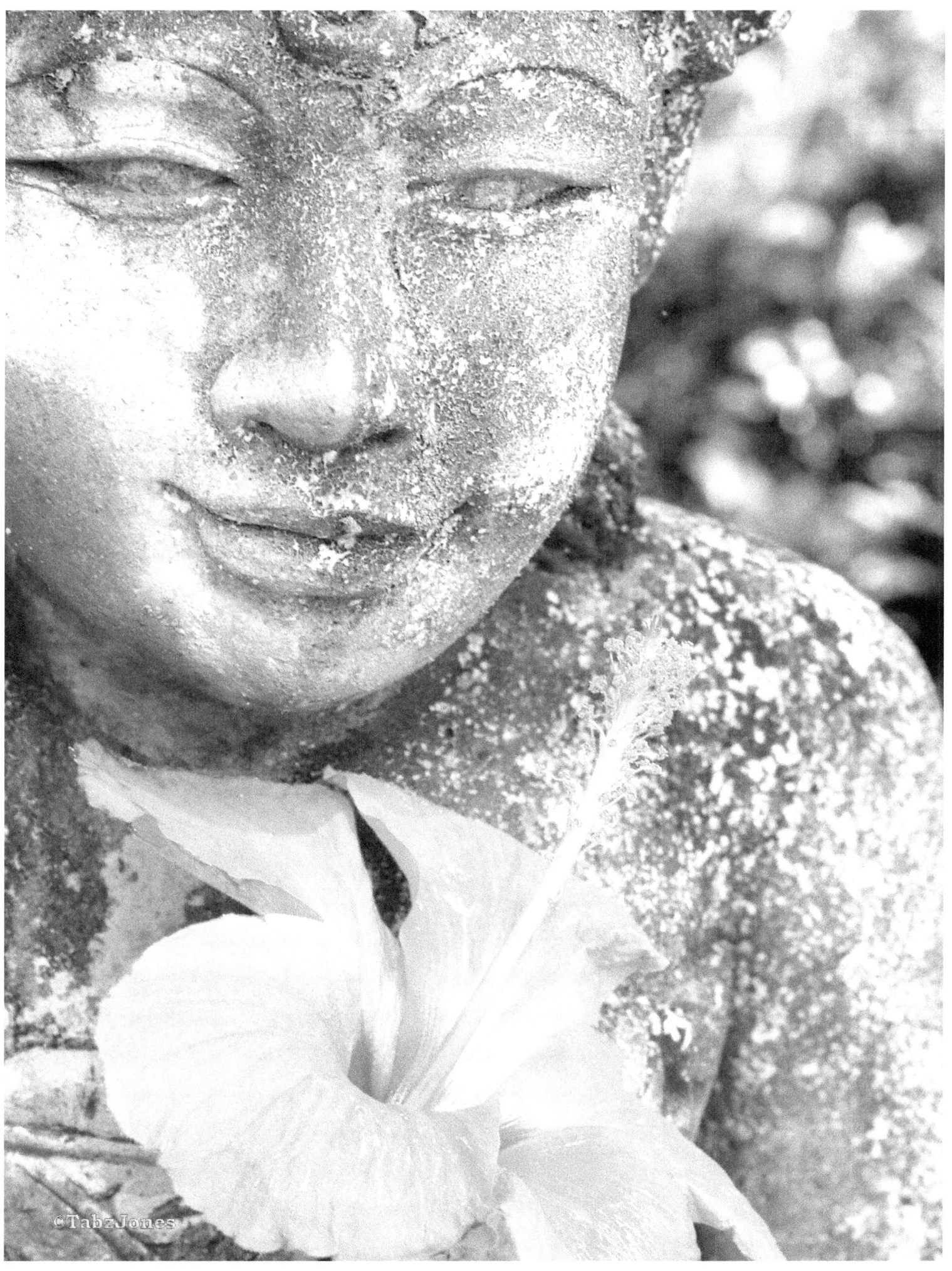

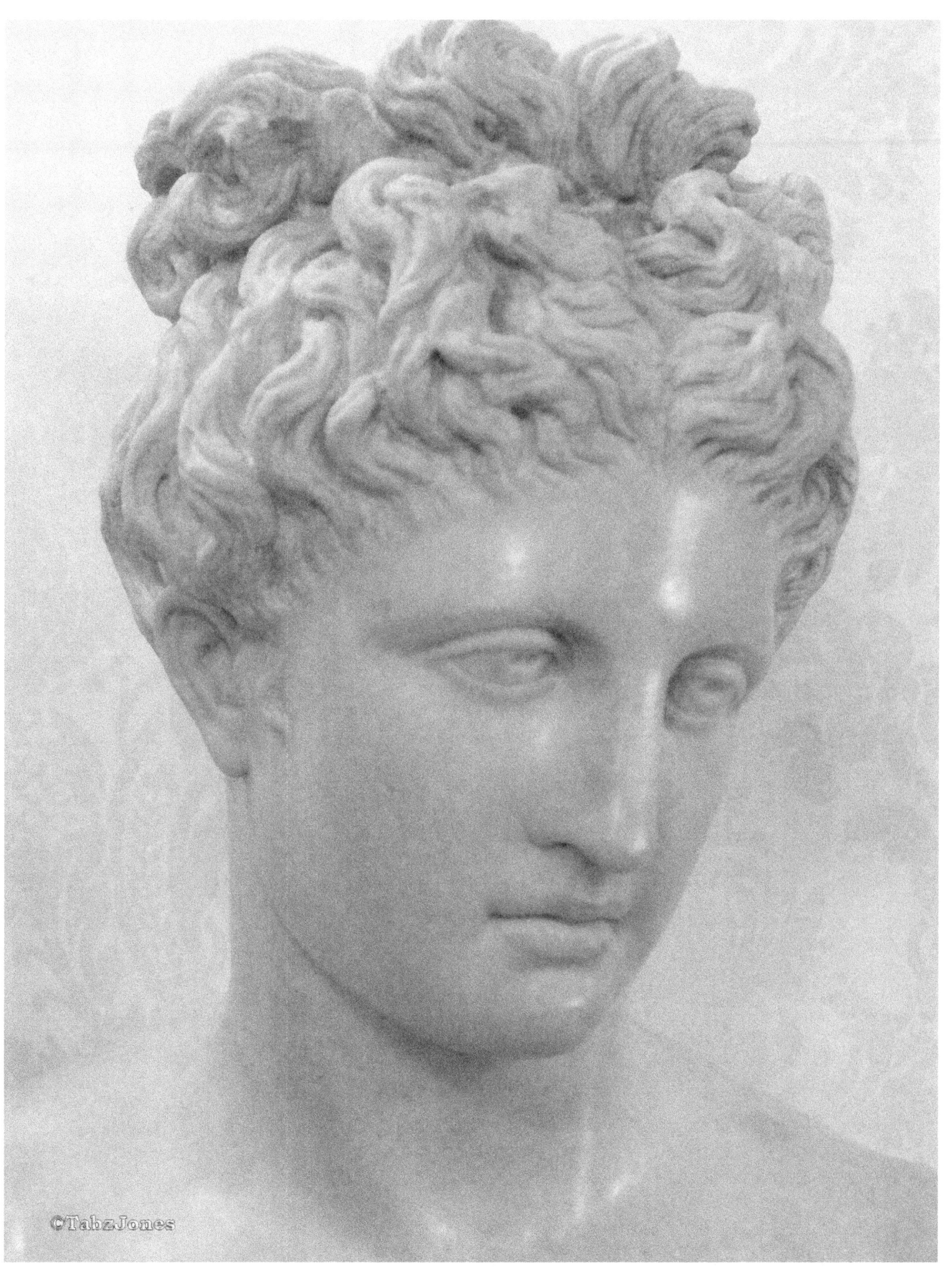

©TabzJones

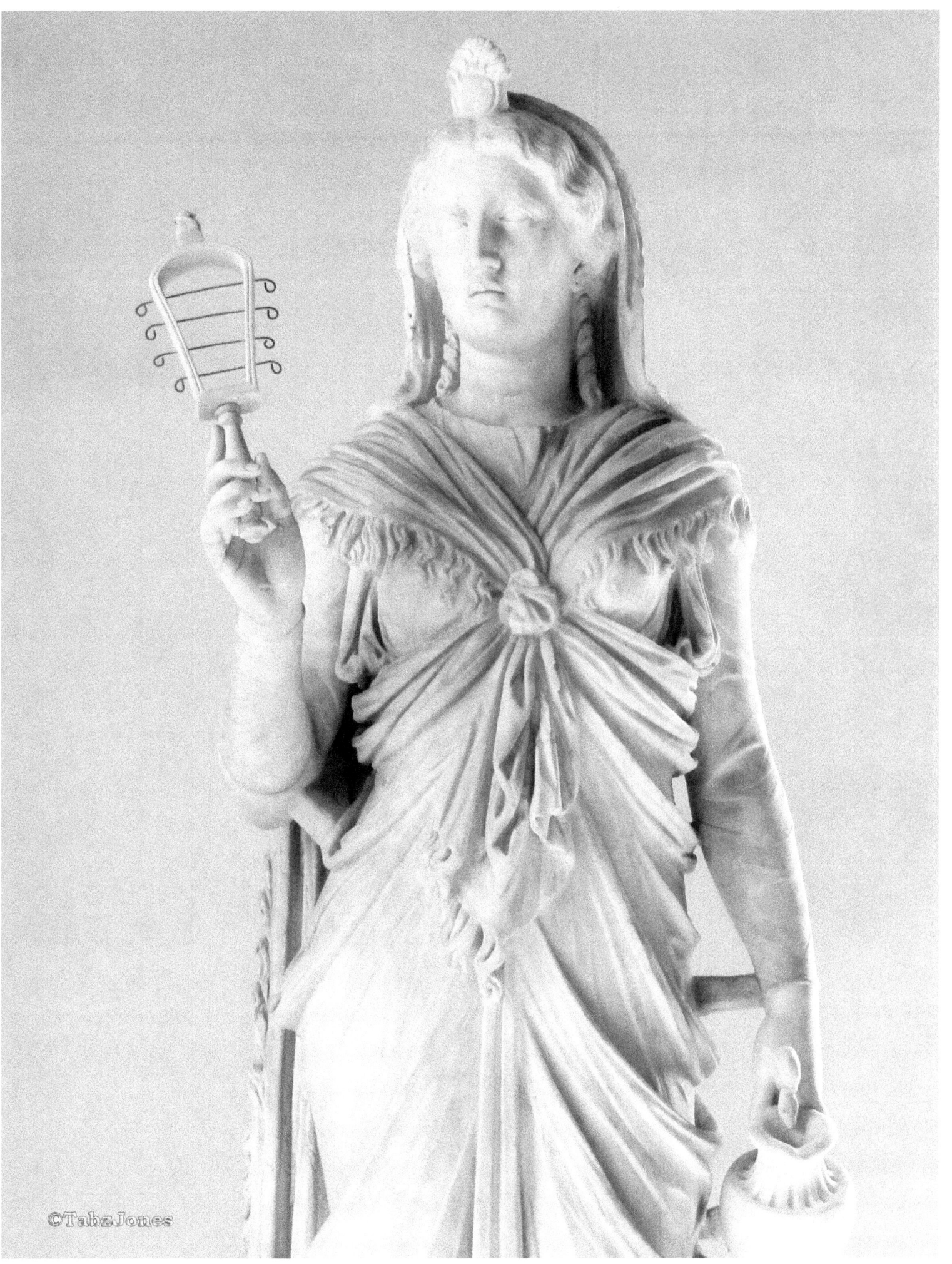

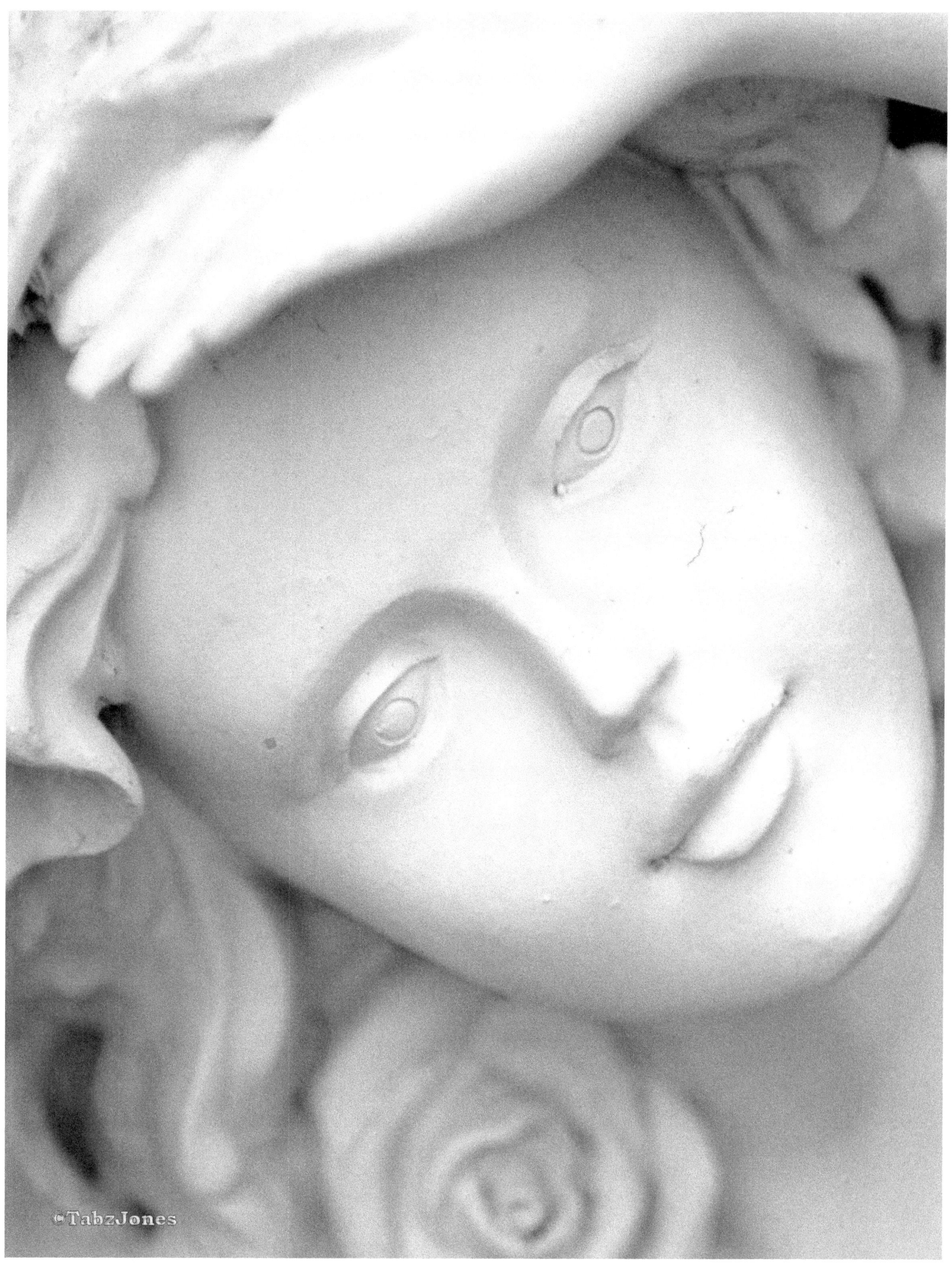
©TabzJones

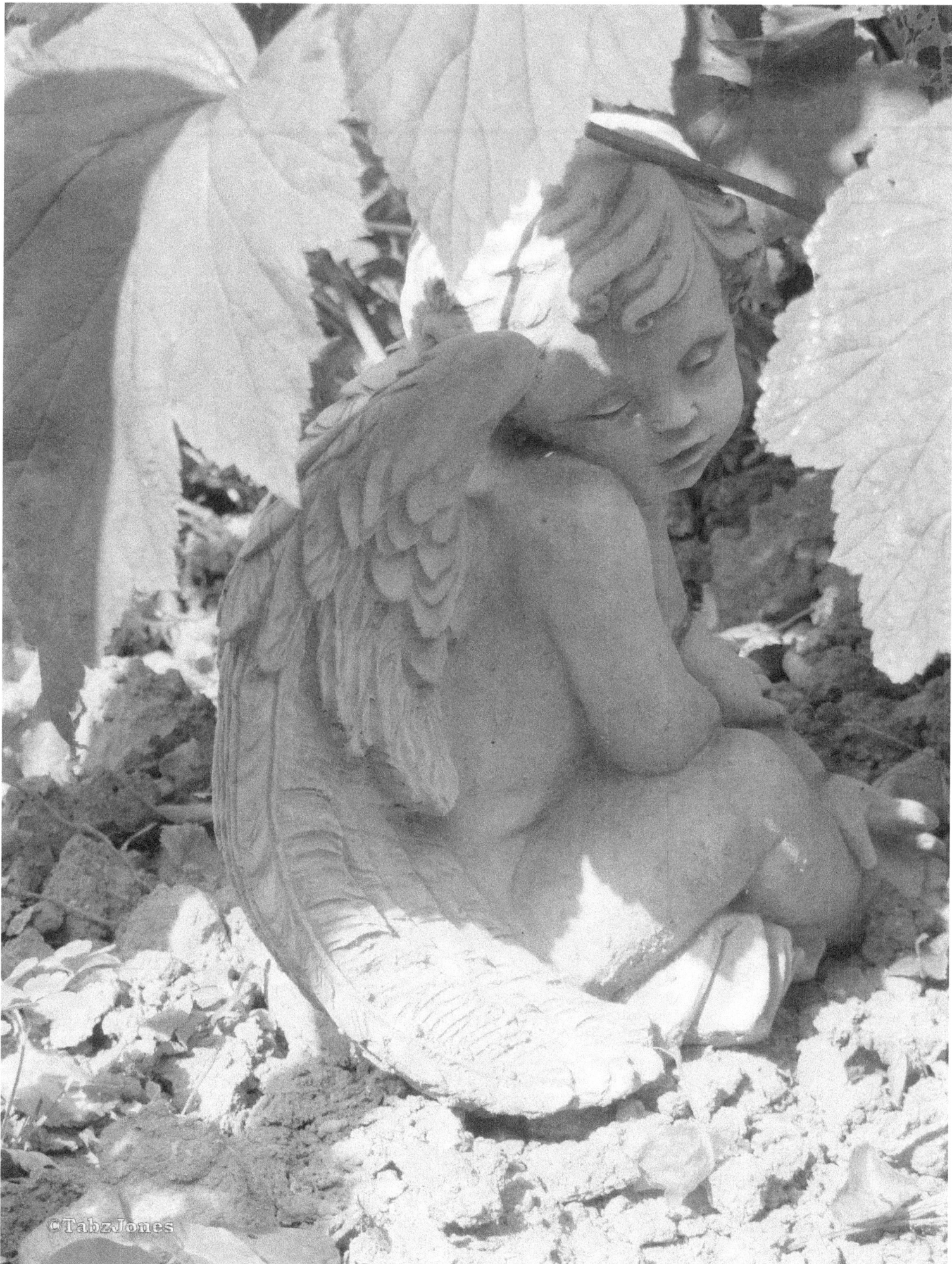

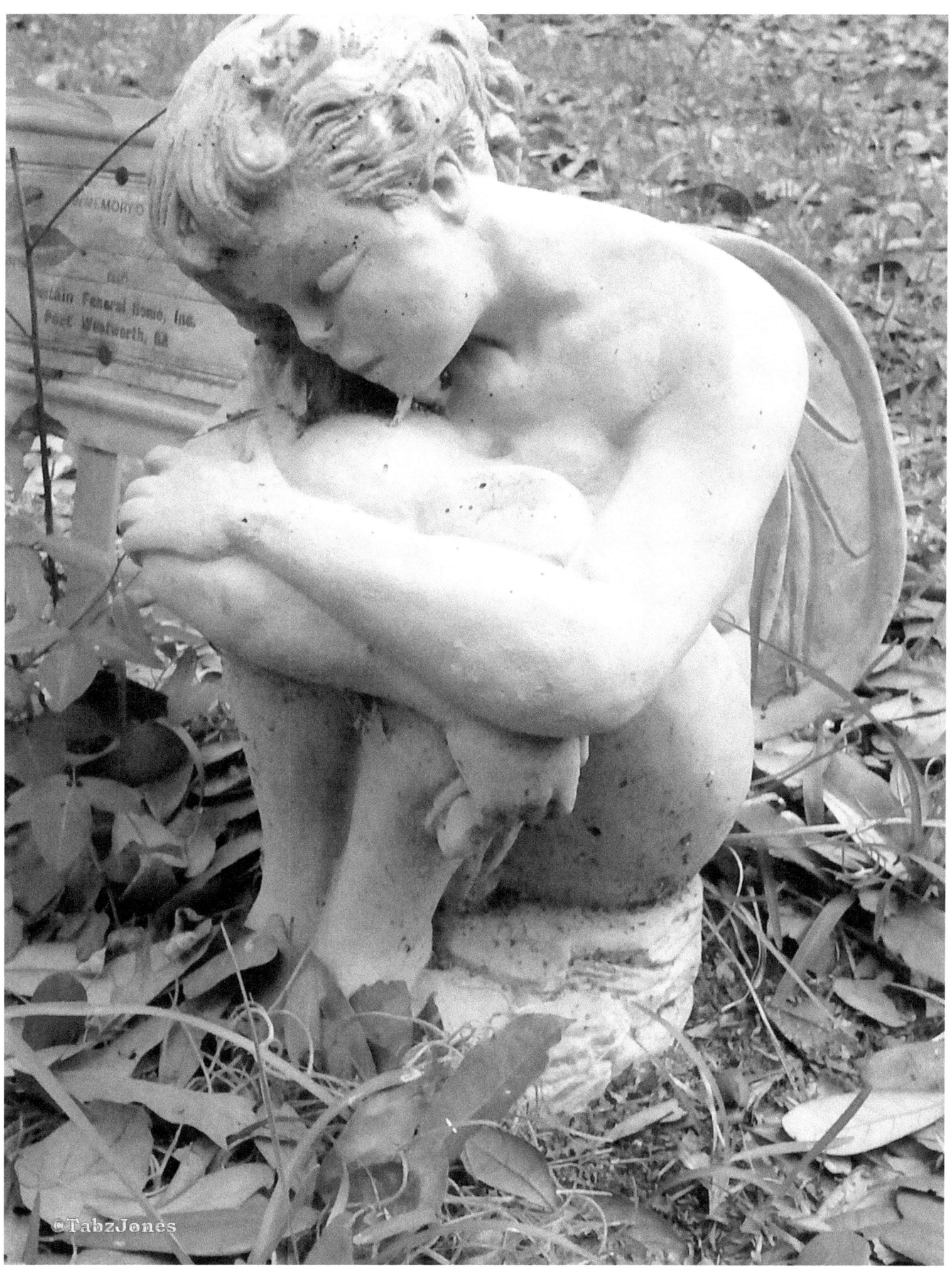

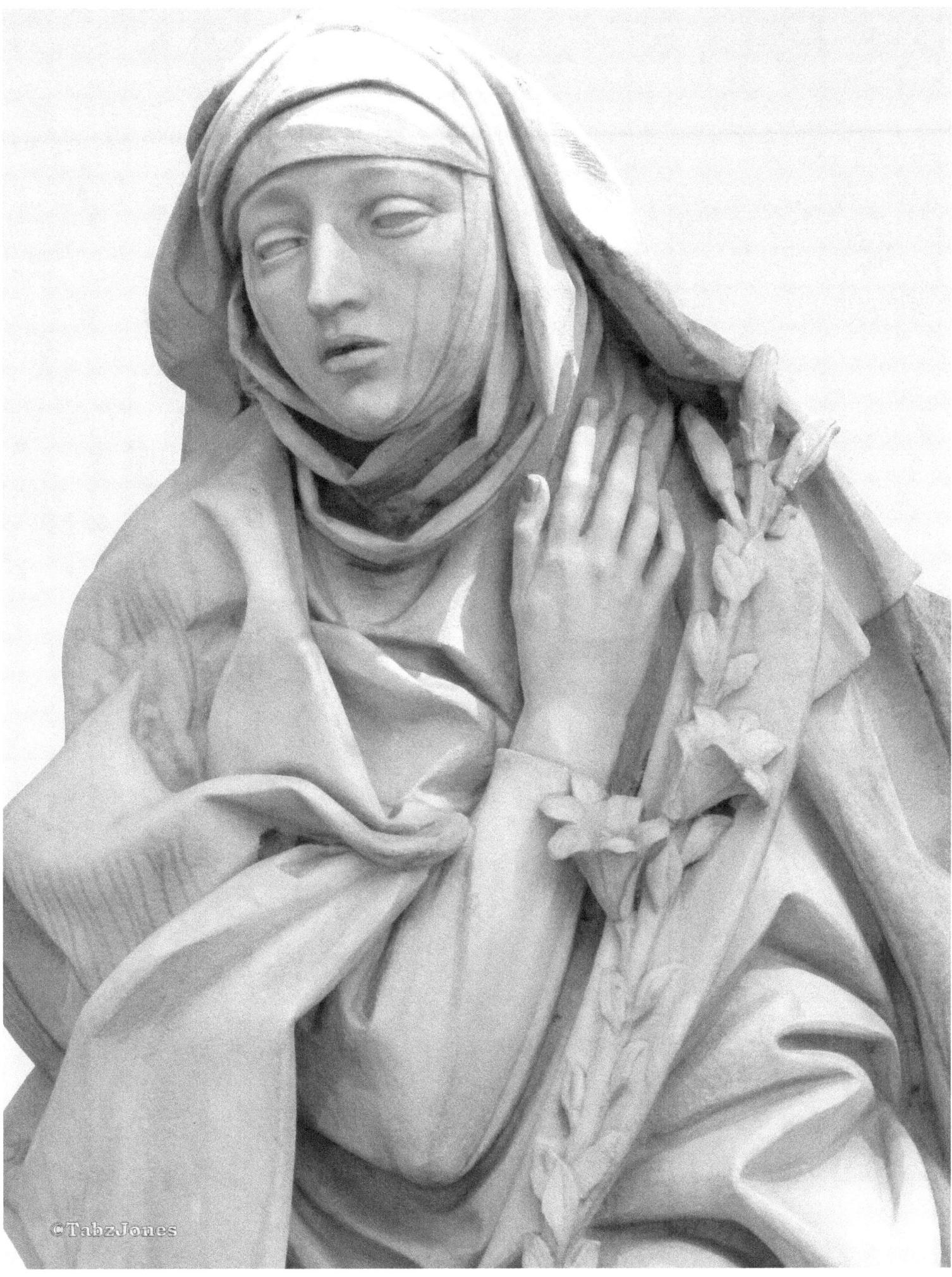
©TabzJones

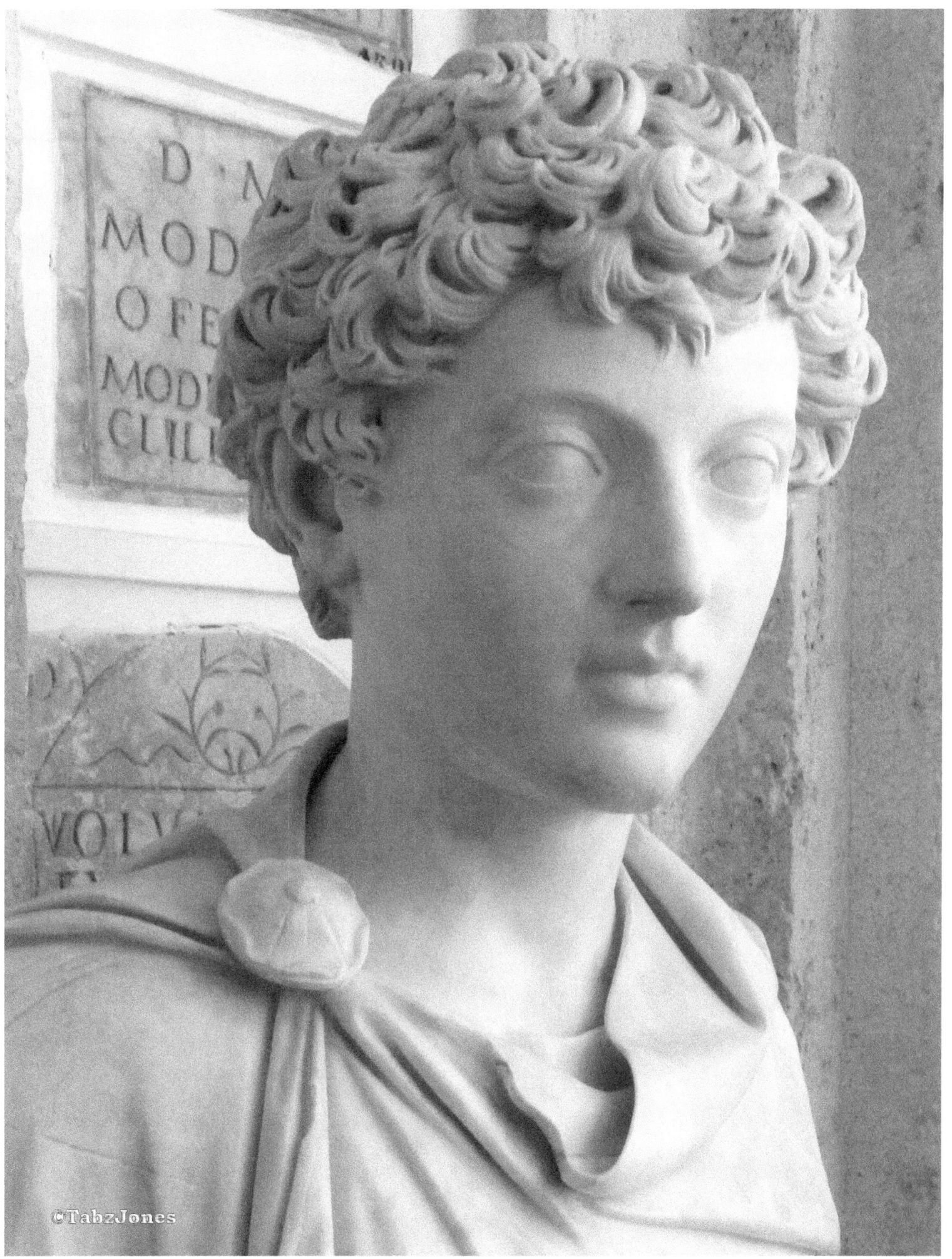

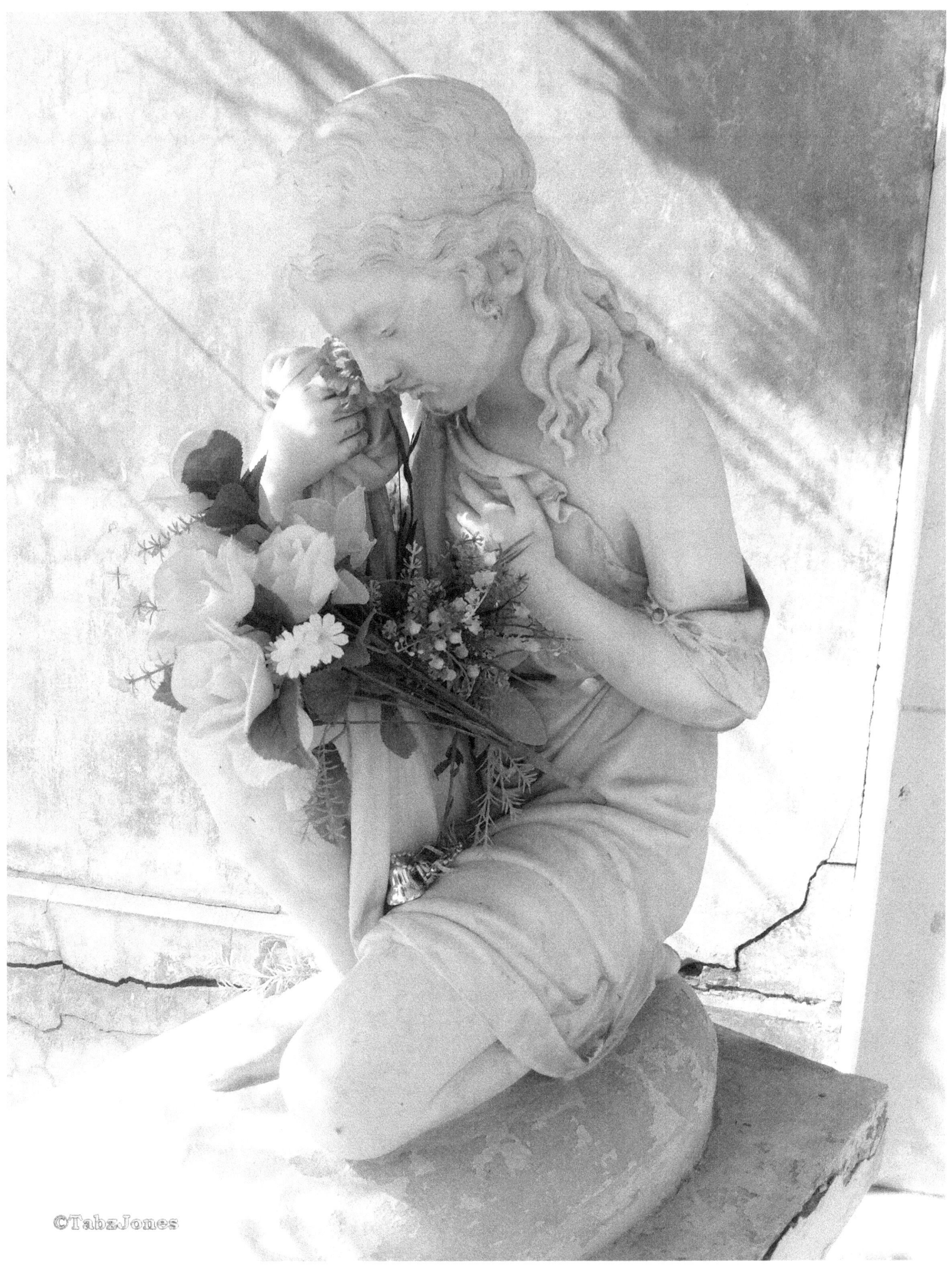
©TabzJones

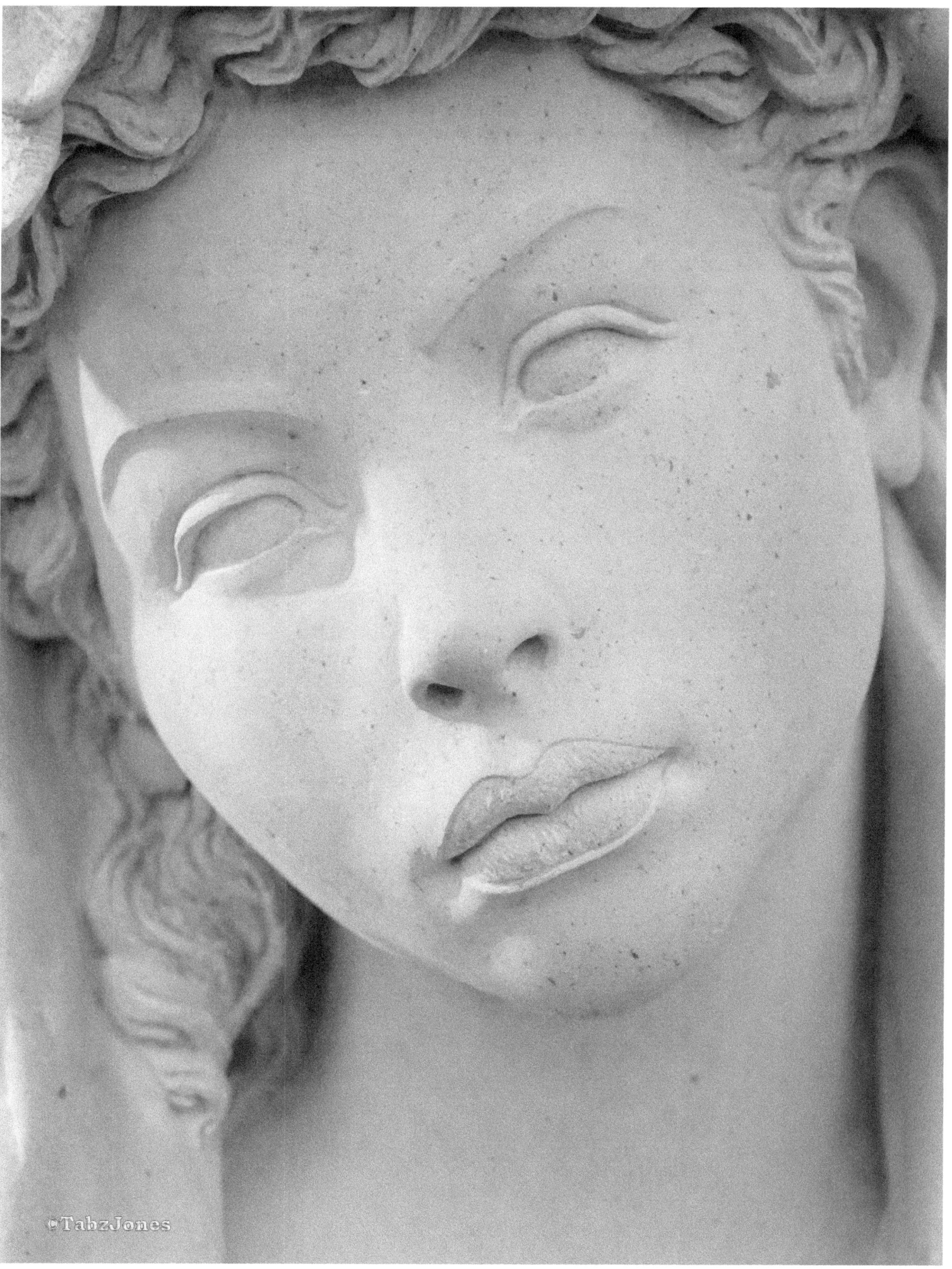

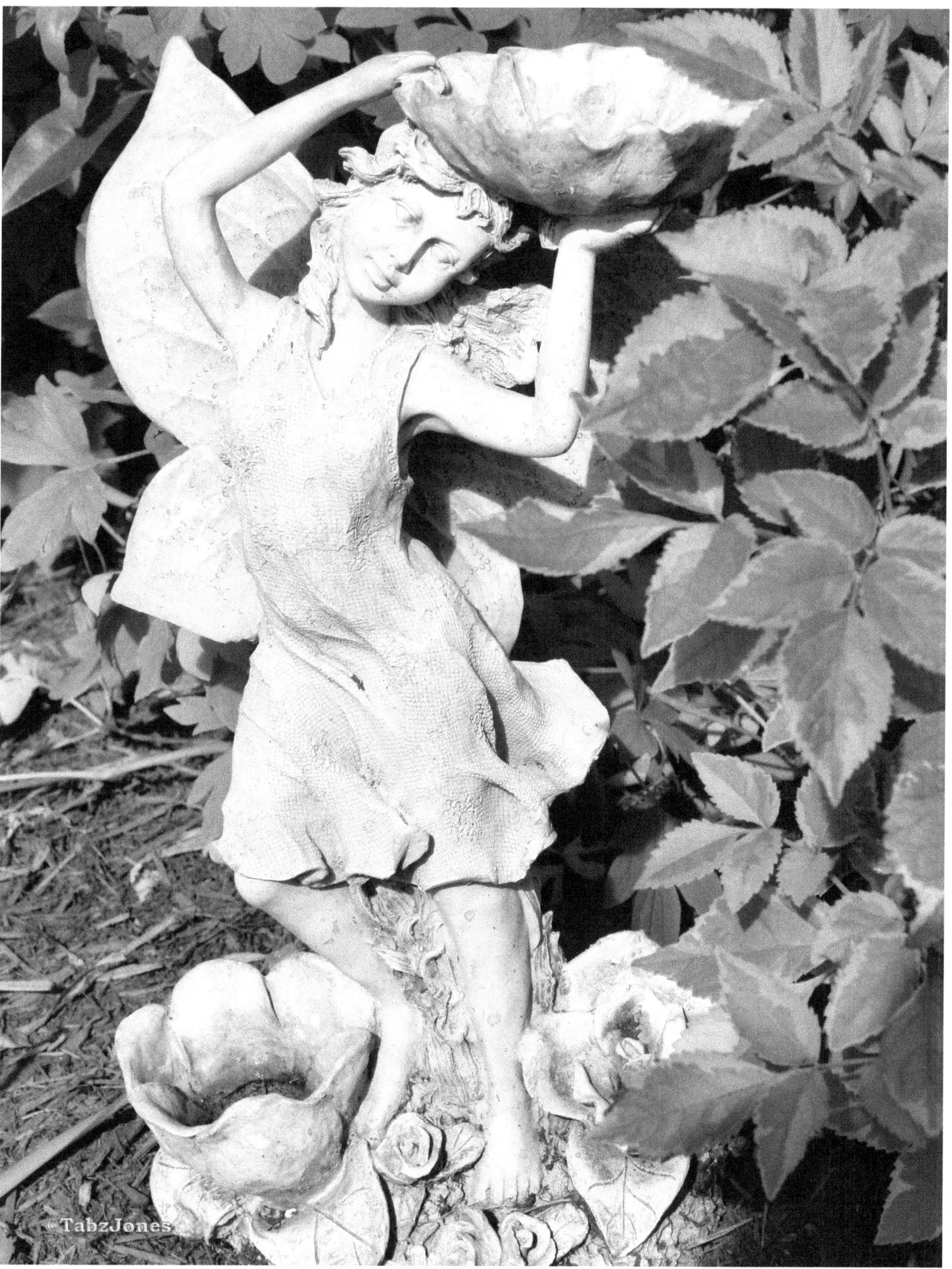

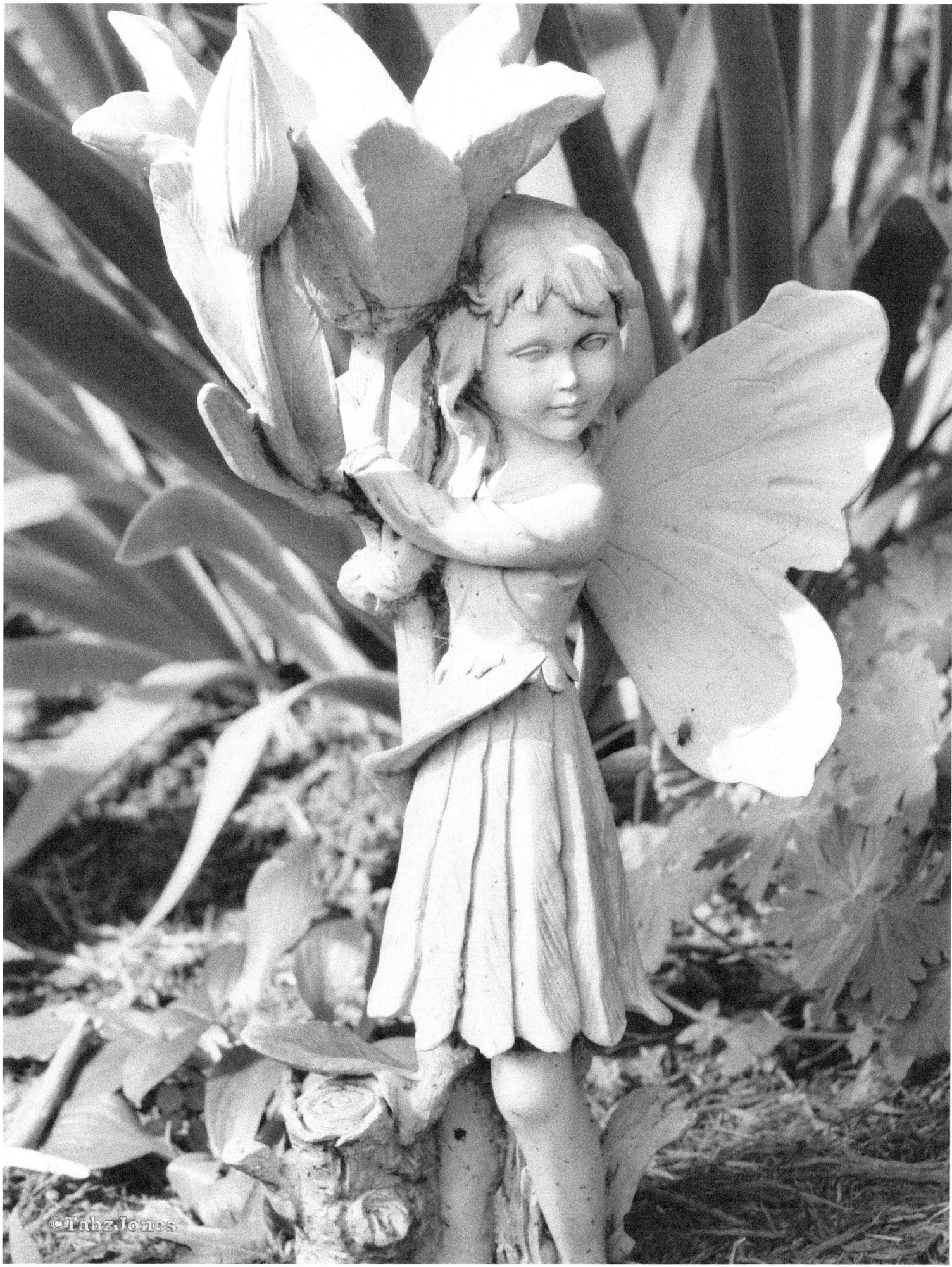

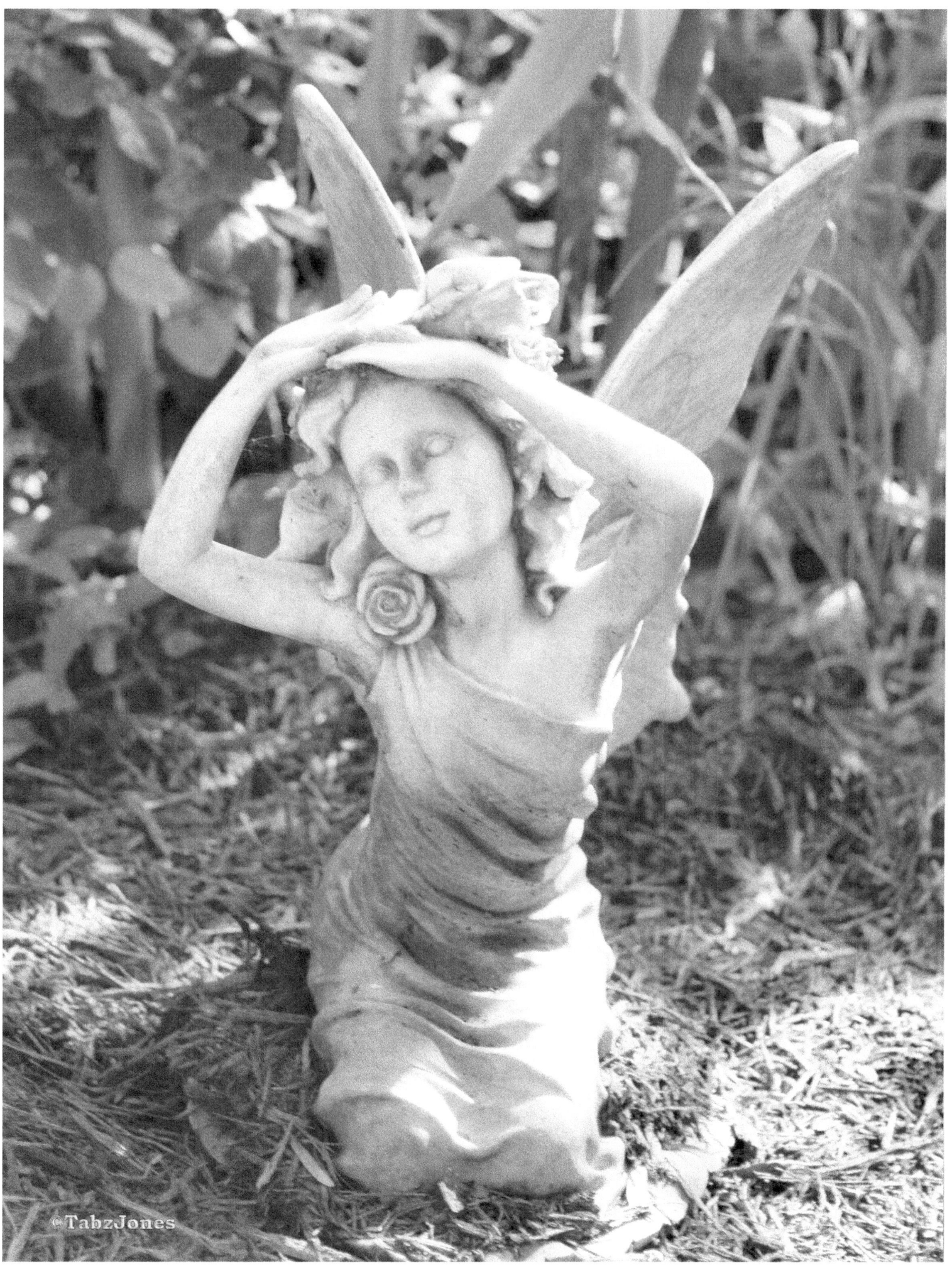

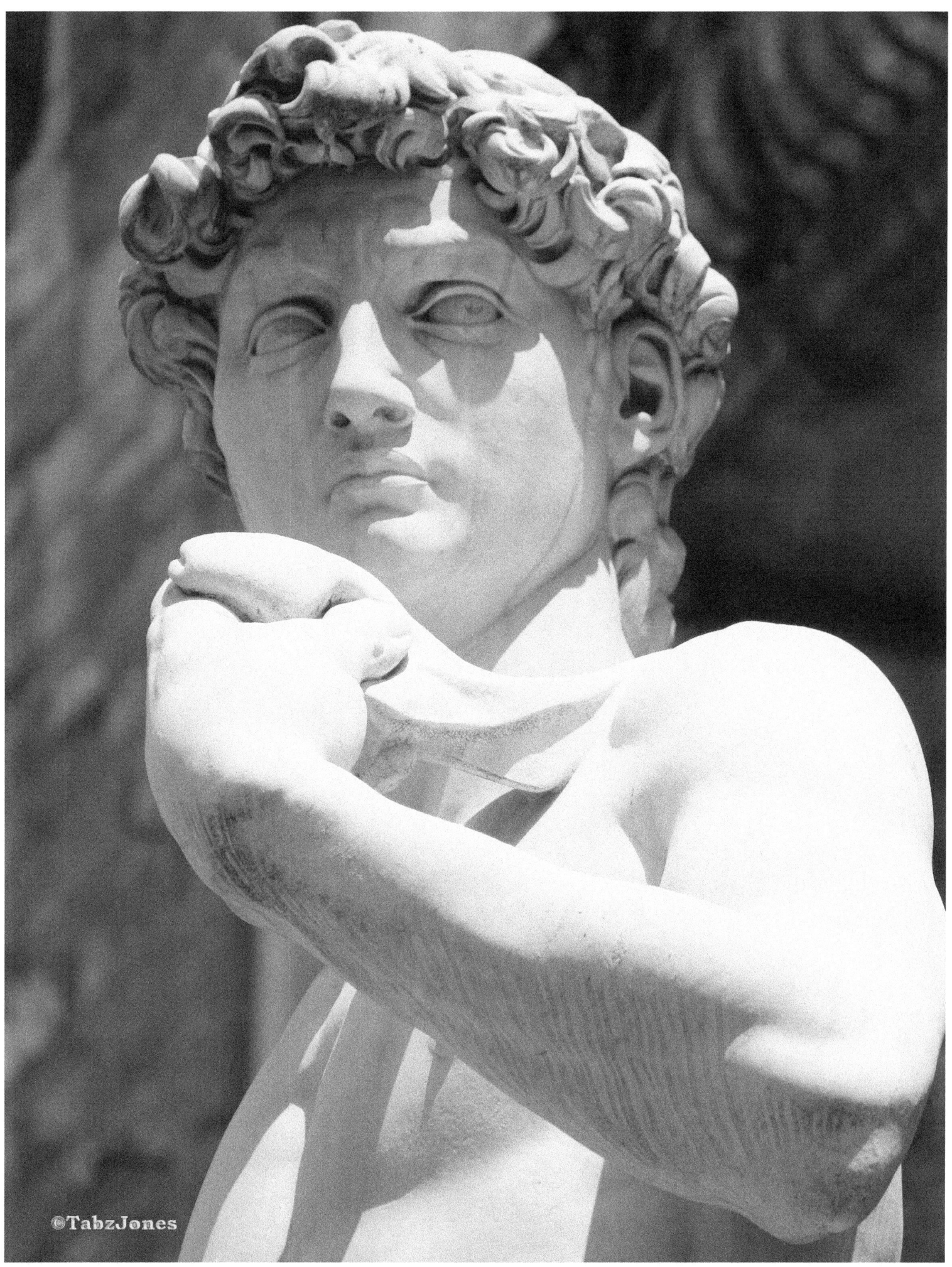

©TabzJones

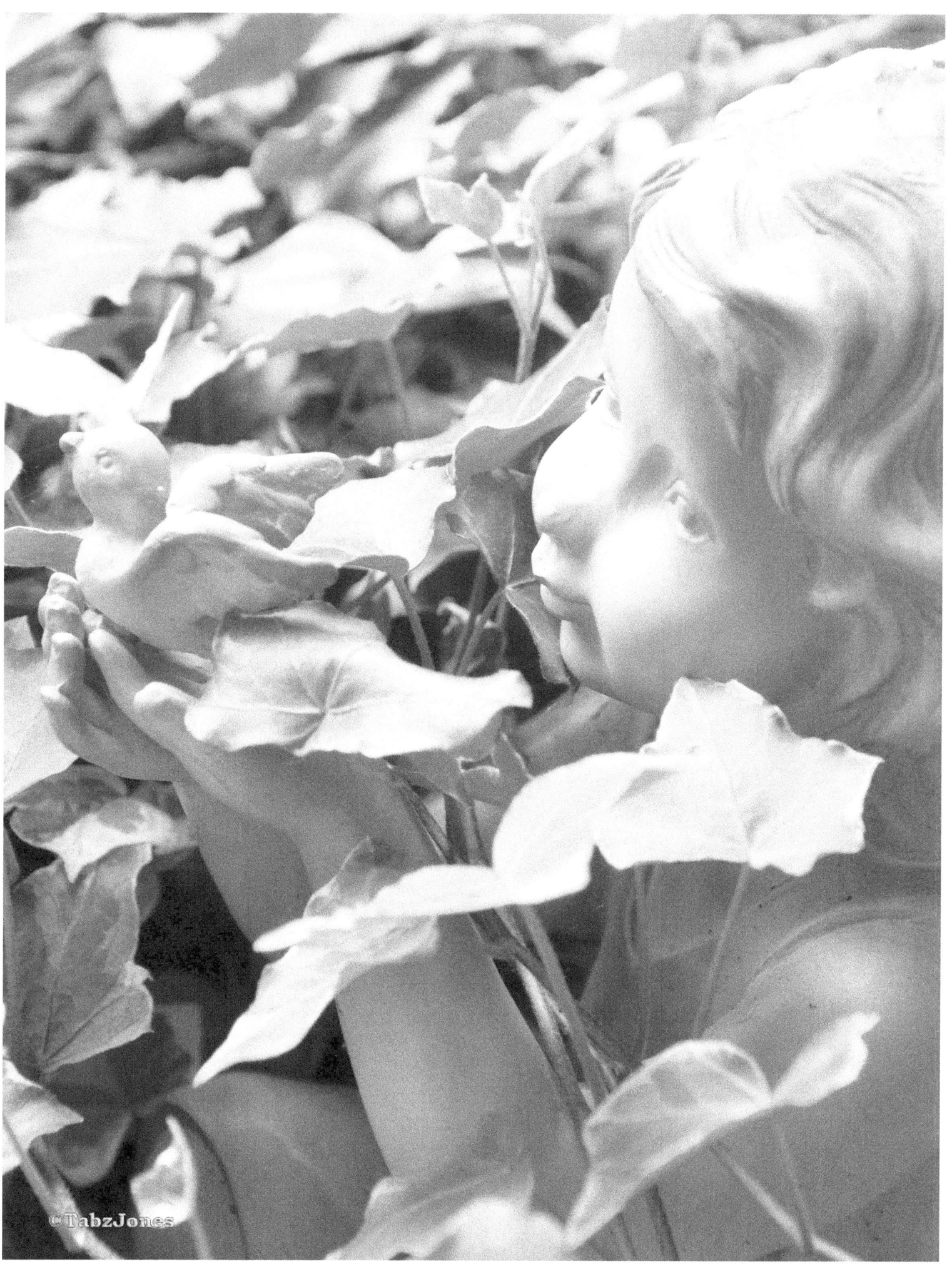
©TabzJones

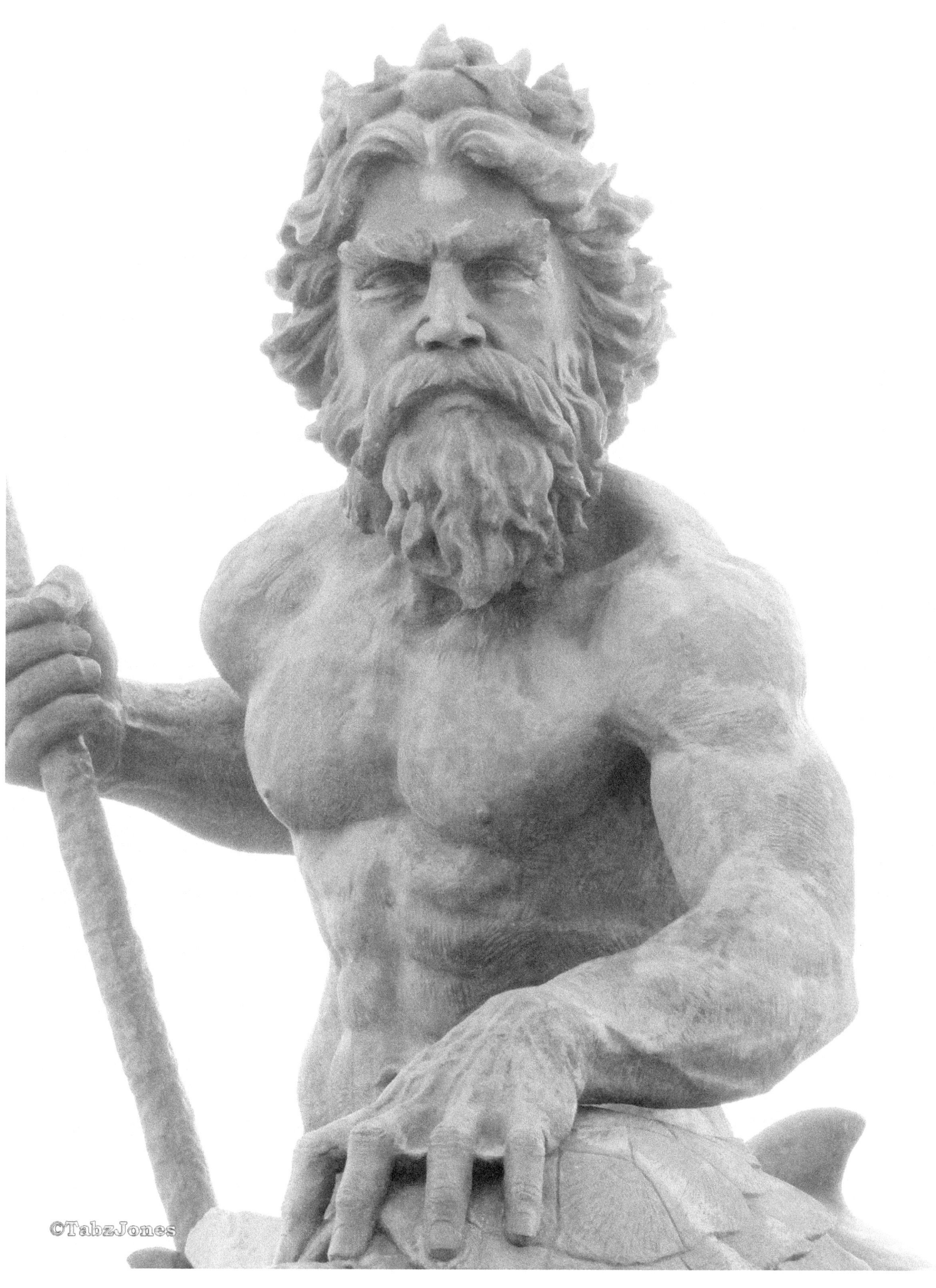

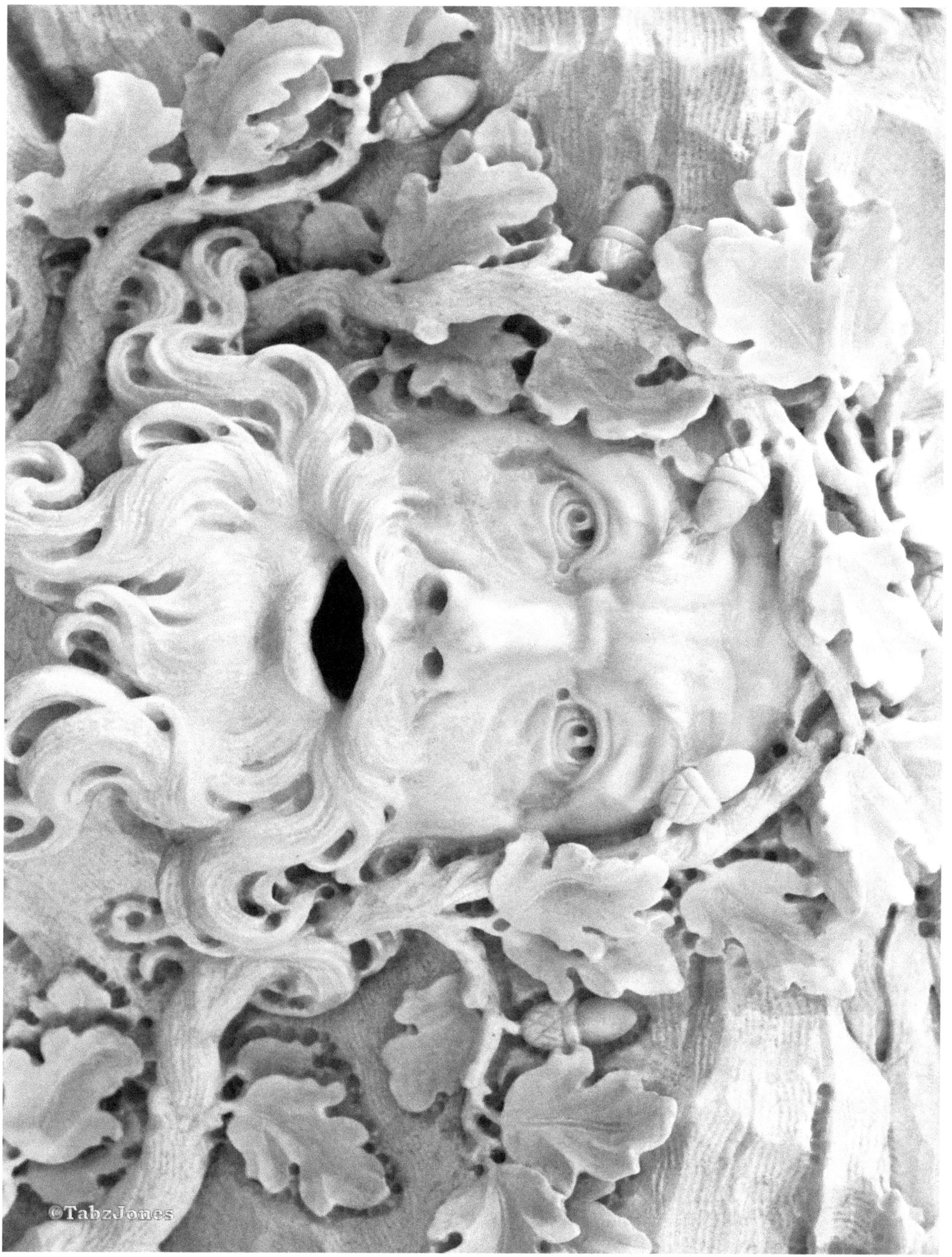
©TabzJones

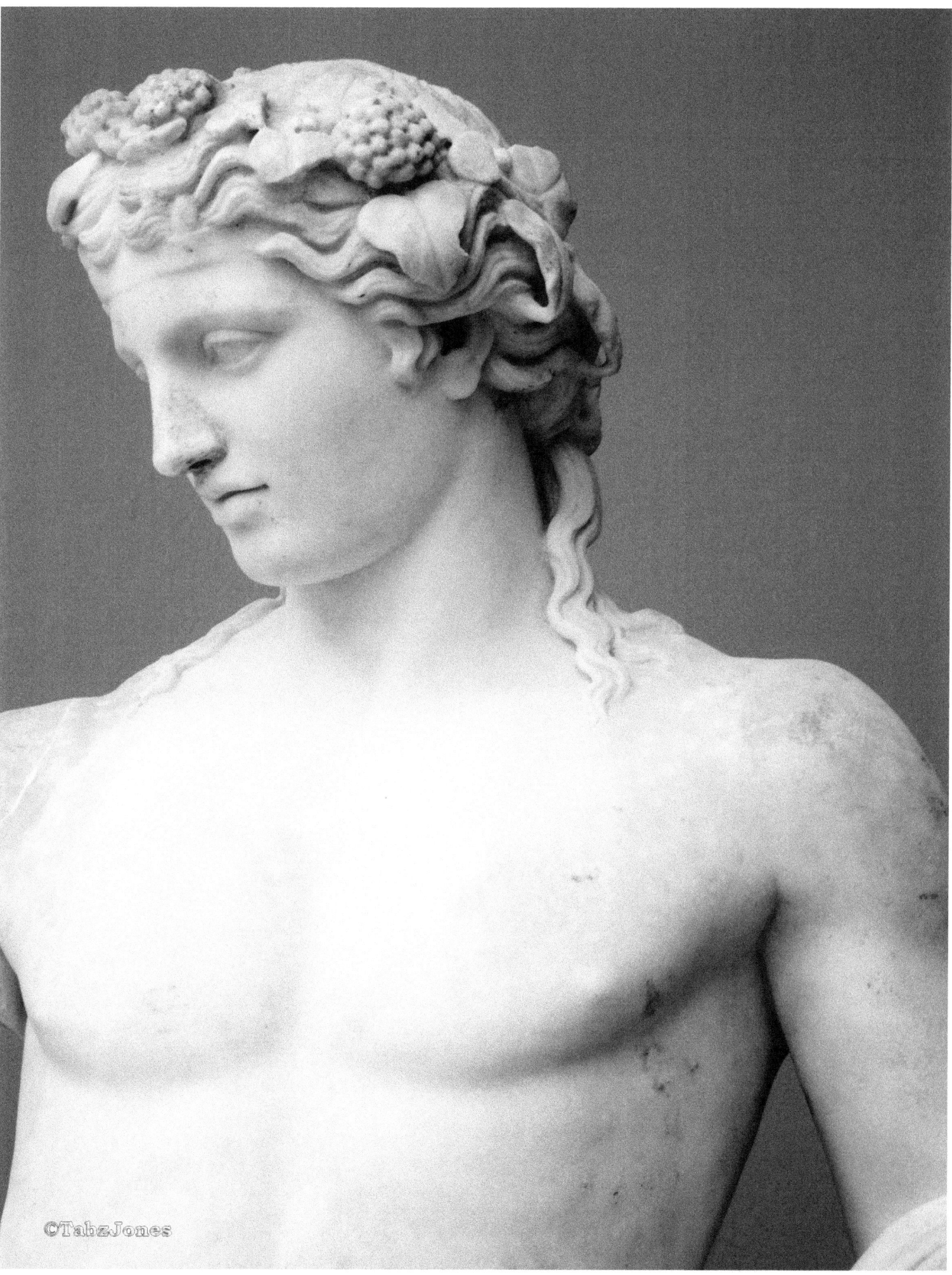

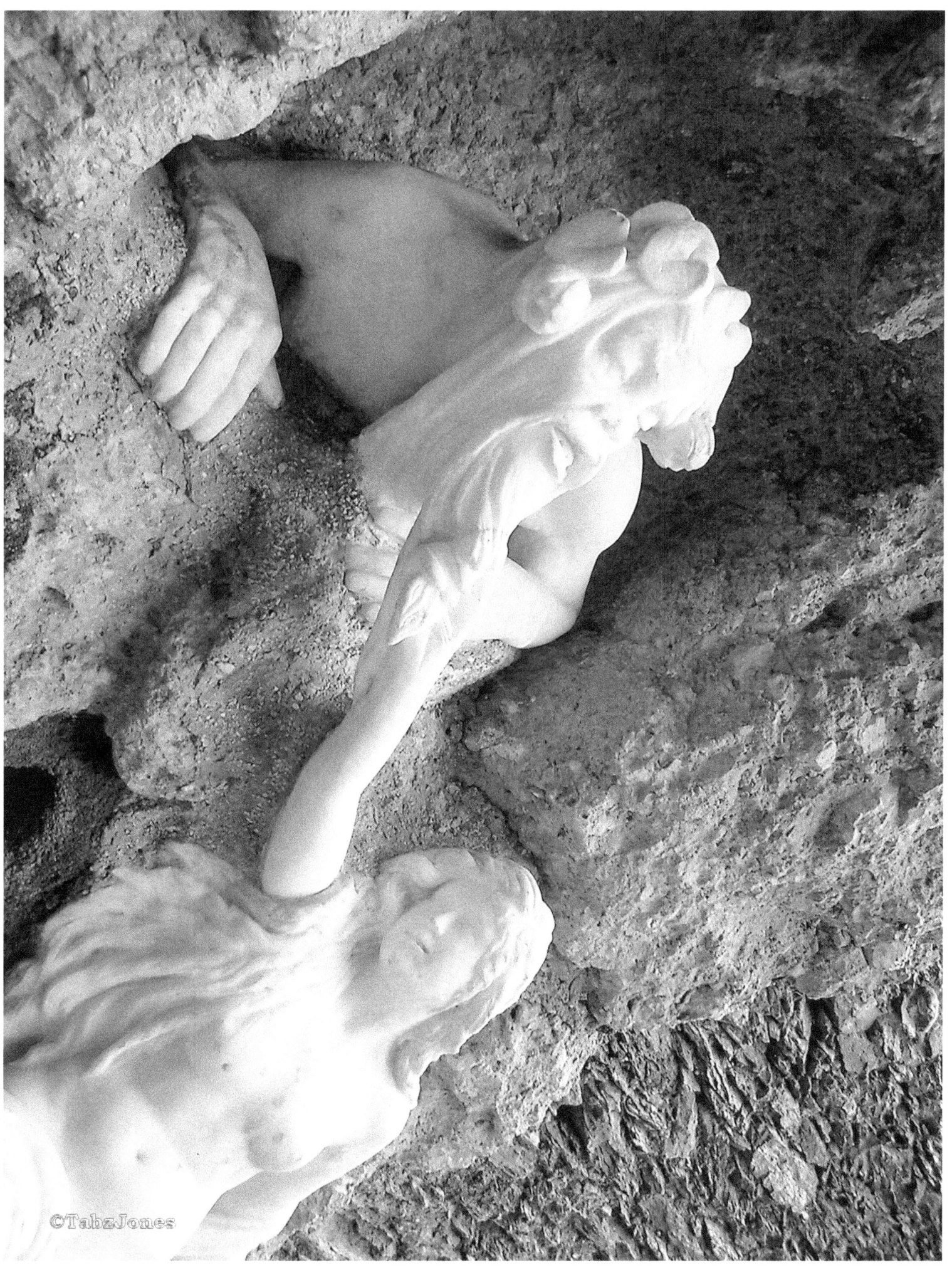

©TabzJones

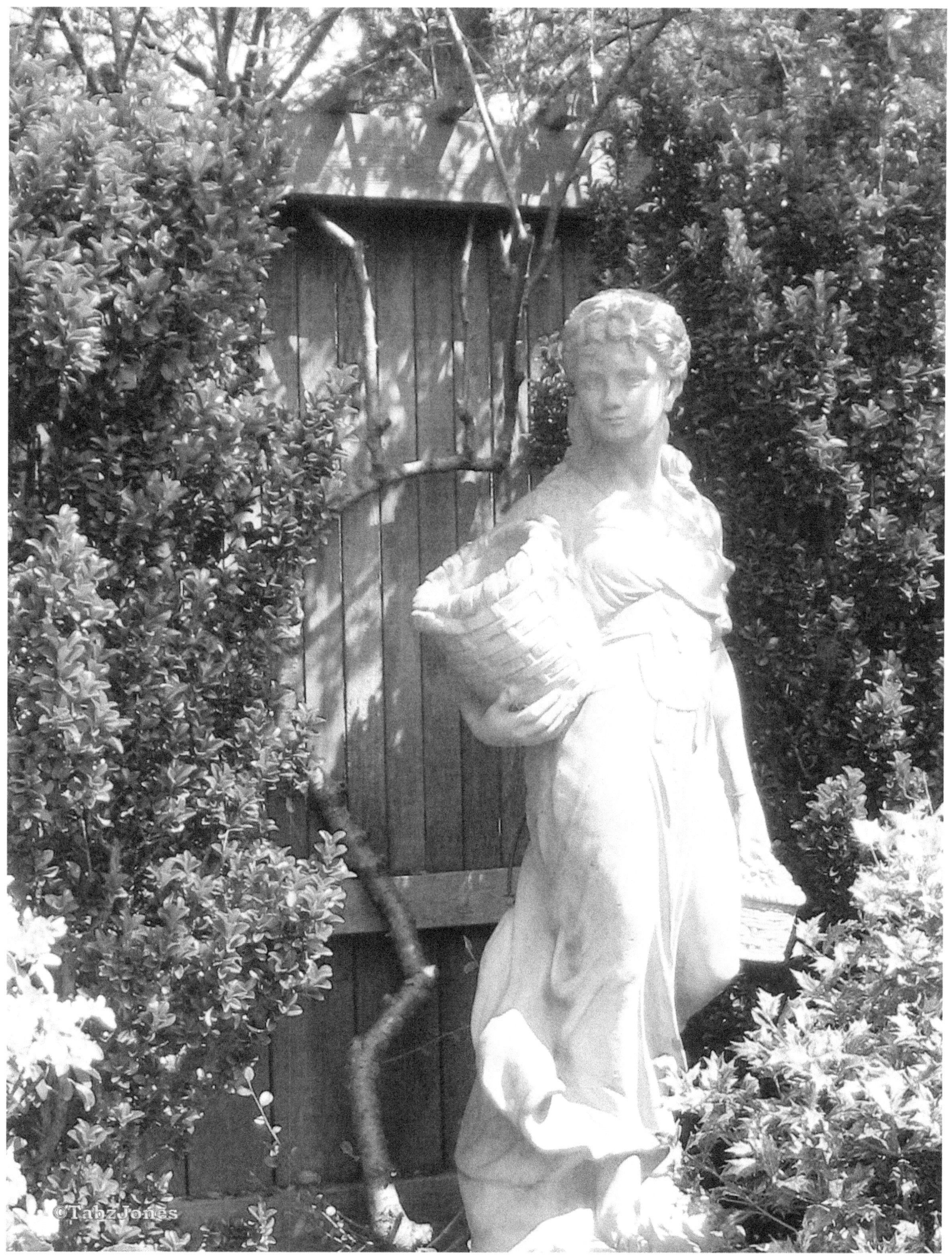

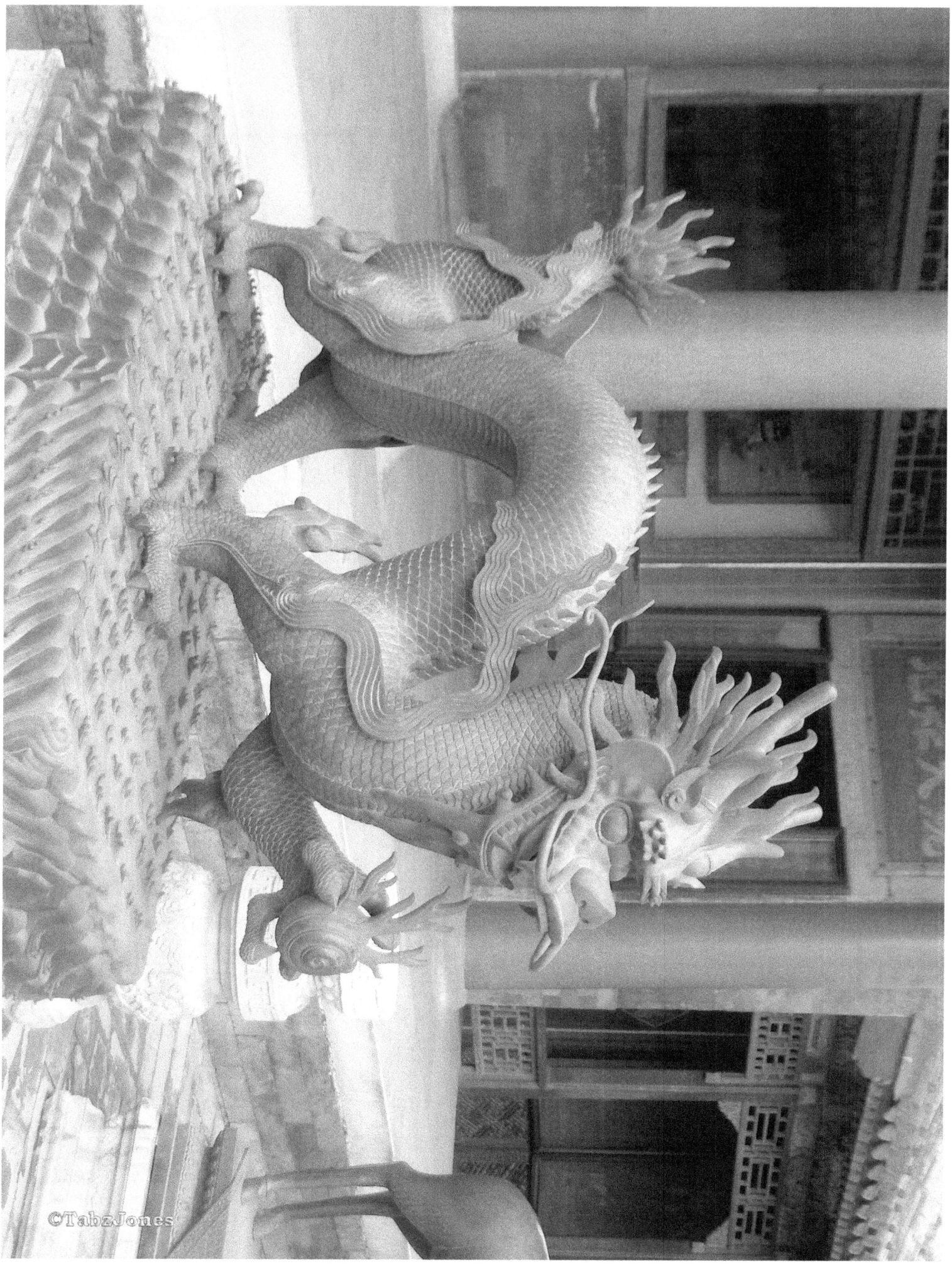
©TabzJones

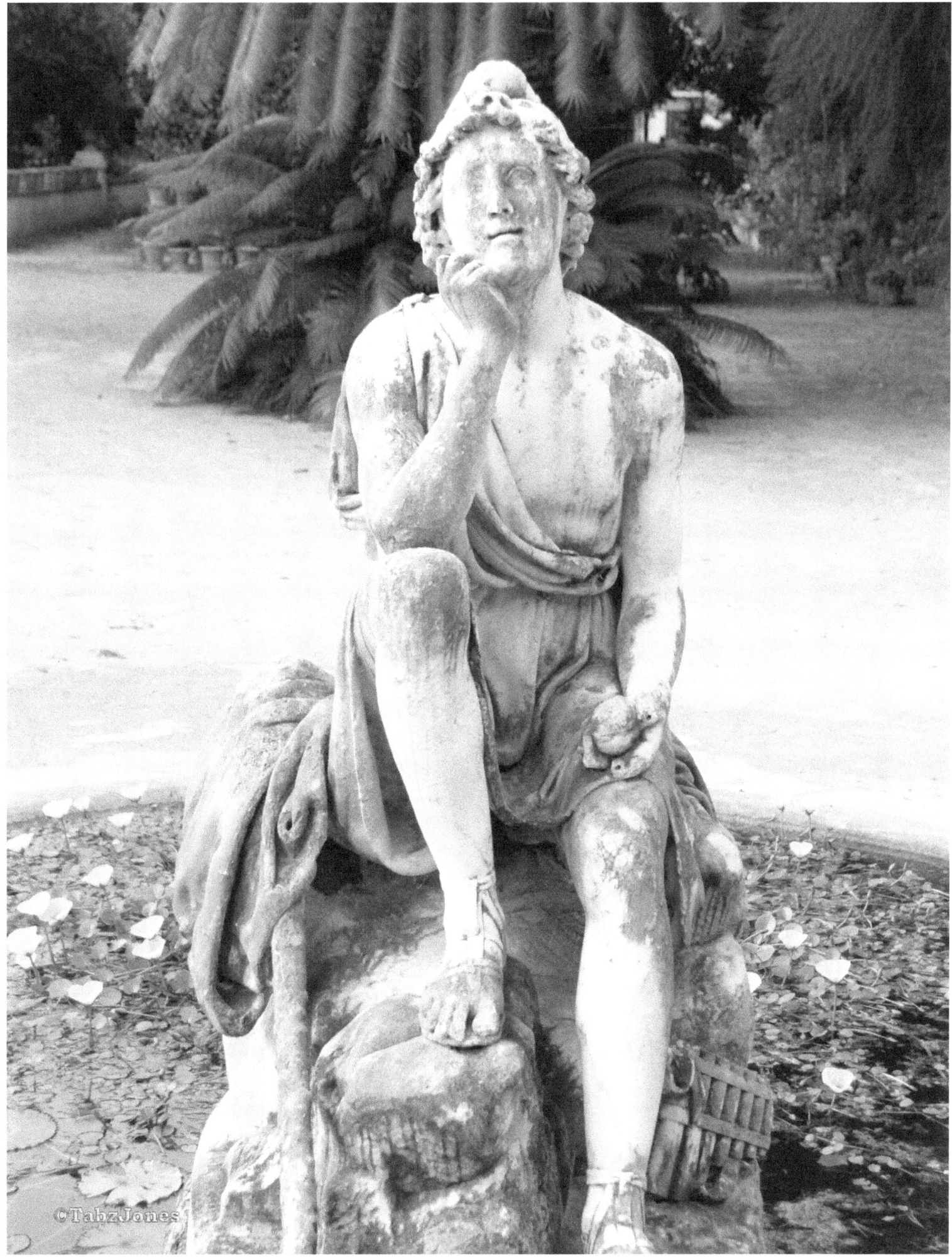

©TabzJones

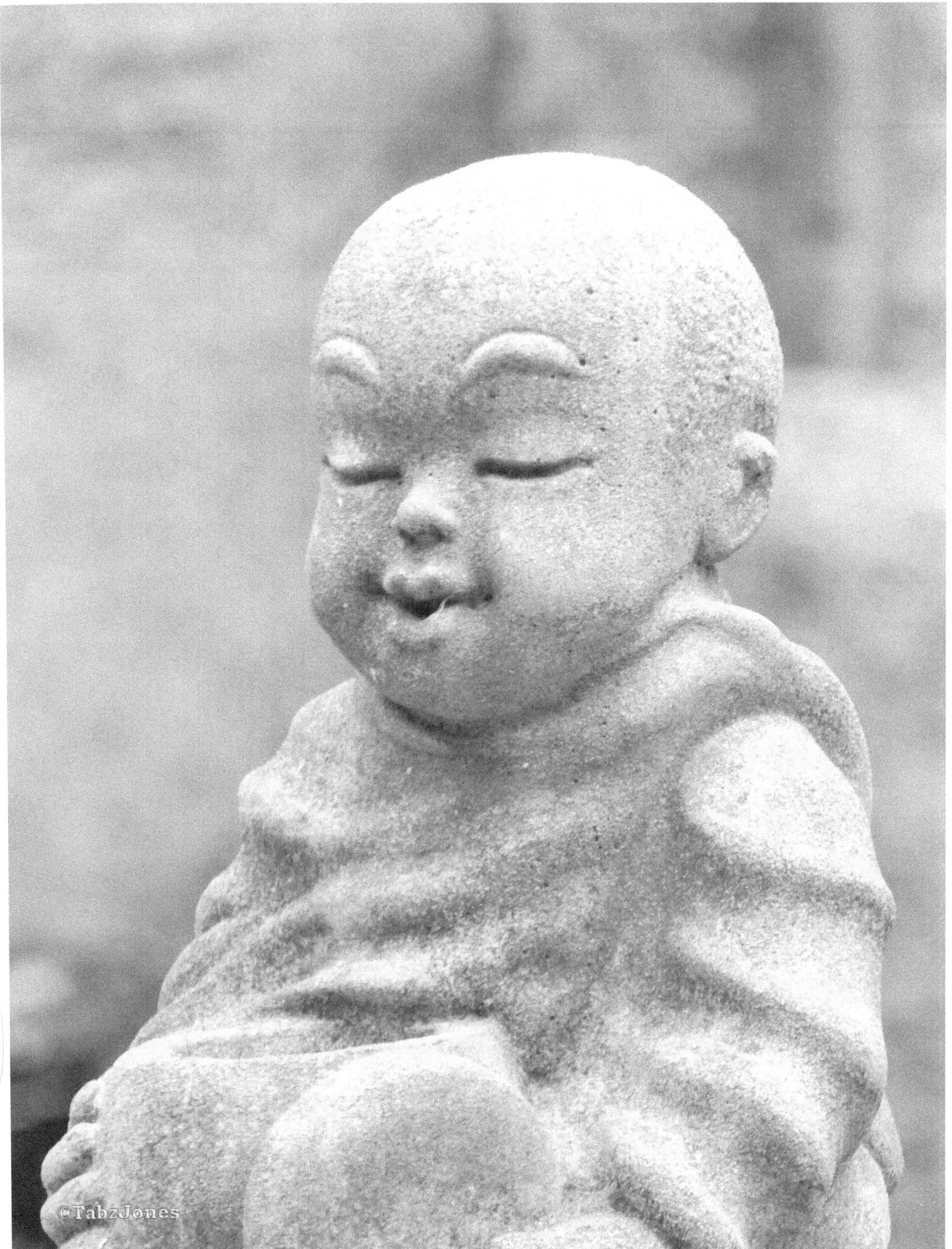

www.ingramcontent.com/pod-product-compliance
Lightning Source LLC
Chambersburg PA
CBHW080605190526
45169CB00007B/2879